D1607366

GOLD
STANDARD

ARTIFACTS
THROUGHOUT AMERICAN HISTORY

BY BARBARA M. LINDE

Gareth Stevens
PUBLISHING

Please visit our website, www.garethstevens.com. For a free color catalog of all our high-quality books, call toll free 1-800-542-2595 or fax 1-877-542-2596.

Library of Congress Cataloging-in-Publication Data

Names: Linde, Barbara M., author.
Title: Artifacts throughout American history / Barbara M. Linde.
Description: New York : Gareth Stevens Publishing, [2020] | Series: Journey to the past : investigating primary sources | Includes bibliographical references and index.
Identifiers: LCCN 2018058561| ISBN 9781538240304 (pbk.) | ISBN 9781538240328 (library bound) | ISBN 9781538240311 (6 pack)
Subjects: LCSH: United States--History--Juvenile literature. | United States--Antiquities--Juvenile literature. | Material culture--United States--Juvenile literature. | United States--Social life and customs--Juvenile literature.
Classification: LCC E178.3 .L56 2020 | DDC 973--dc23
LC record available at https://lccn.loc.gov/2018058561

First Edition

Published in 2020 by
Gareth Stevens Publishing
111 East 14th Street, Suite 349
New York, NY 10003

Copyright © 2020 Gareth Stevens Publishing

Designer: Katelyn E. Reynolds
Editor: Jill Keppeler

CONTENTS

WORDS IN THE GLOSSARY APPEAR IN **BOLD** TYPE
THE FIRST TIME THEY ARE USED IN THE TEXT.

THE IMPORTANCE OF ARTIFACTS

A primary source is a **document** or object that provides firsthand information about something. An artifact is a type of primary source. It's something that people made and used. A piece of pottery, a toy, or a coin from the past are all artifacts. Some people saved these things, and some threw them away. Changes in the land or new construction buried some older artifacts.

When archaeologists, historians, or others find an artifact, they try to figure out what time period it's from and how it related to that time period. They may compare artifacts from the same time and location, from different times, or from different **cultures.** Learning about artifacts helps us find out how people before us lived and worked.

ANALYZE IT!

WASHINGTON'S TENT WAS HIS HEADQUARTERS AND SLEEPING AREA. IT WAS PITCHED ALONGSIDE THOSE OF HIS TROOPS. WHAT COULD IT TELL YOU ABOUT HIS LIFE AND THAT OF THE SOLDIERS DURING THE WAR?

HOW TO ANALYZE AN ARTIFACT

WHEN YOU **ANALYZE** AN ARTIFACT, YOU ASK QUESTIONS TO FIND OUT MORE ABOUT IT. YOUR QUESTIONS MIGHT INCLUDE: WHO MADE THIS? WHO USED THIS? WHAT IS IT MADE OF? WHY WAS THIS IMPORTANT? YOU MIGHT COMPARE THE ARTIFACT WITH SIMILAR ARTIFACTS FROM THAT CULTURE OR ANOTHER CULTURE.

GENERAL GEORGE WASHINGTON'S TENT FROM THE REVOLUTIONARY WAR, SHOWN, IS NOW AT THE MUSEUM OF THE AMERICAN REVOLUTION IN PHILADELPHIA, PENNSYLVANIA.

THE FIRST ENGLISH SETTLERS

The first permanent English settlement in North America began at Jamestown, Virginia, in 1607. The settlers built a fort and planted crops. The settlement had ups and downs, but in time the population grew. The settlers spread out farther from James Fort. In 1699, the government moved a few miles inland to Williamsburg. James Fort was abandoned for many years.

A metal horse and windmill were excavated from the remains of the fort. Archaeologists compared the toys with written documents from the period. The toys probably were made in England in the early 17th century and brought to Jamestown. Archaeologists don't know who owned or played with the toys. Since there weren't many children in Jamestown's early days, soldiers may have owned these artifacts.

ANALYZE IT!

WHAT ELSE DO YOU WANT TO KNOW ABOUT THESE ARTIFACTS? WHY DO YOU THINK SOLDIERS MAY HAVE OWNED THE TOY SOLDIER AND THE TOY WINDMILL?

PRESERVATION VIRGINIA

IN 1994, THE PRESERVATION VIRGINIA GROUP BEGAN
THE JAMESTOWN REDISCOVERY ARCHAEOLOGICAL DIG.
SO FAR, RESEARCHERS HAVE FOUND THE SITE OF THE FORT,
REMAINS OF SOME OF THE ORIGINAL BUILDINGS, AND OVER 1.5 MILLION
ARTIFACTS. MANY OF THESE ARTIFACTS ARE ON DISPLAY AT THE MUSEUM
IN JAMESTOWN.

SOME OF THE ITEMS FOUND AT THE DIG INCLUDE CONTAINERS, SHOES,
ARMOR, JUGS, FISHHOOKS, AND NATIVE AMERICAN ARTIFACTS.

SHIRTS AND SYMBOLS

Hunters from the area west of the Blue Ridge Mountains in North America were the first to wear a distinctive type of fringed hunting shirt. Some historians think the style was modeled after Native American shirts. As the American Revolution approached, some hunters wore the shirts as a unified sign of **rebellion** against Great Britain.

When the Revolution started, many of these expert riflemen from Virginia, Maryland, and Pennsylvania marched to Boston to join the Continental army. Many wore hunting shirts, some with the words "liberty or death" from Patrick Henry's famous speech embroidered on them. General George Washington knew these men's reputation as fierce, exact marksmen. Believing that the sight of the shirts would frighten the British soldiers, Washington encouraged all the Continental army soldiers to wear hunting shirts.

ANALYZE IT!

WHAT DOES WASHINGTON'S USE OF THE HUNTING SHIRTS SAY ABOUT HIS SKILL AS A MILITARY LEADER? HOW CAN AN ITEM OF CLOTHING BECOME A SYMBOL OF A MOVEMENT?

LOTS OF VARIETY

HUNTING SHIRTS WERE ONLY ONE TYPE OF ITEM WORN
DURING THE REVOLUTION. ESPECIALLY IN THE BEGINNING, THE
SOLDIERS WORE MANY DIFFERENT TYPES OF UNIFORMS. LATER, THEIR
UNIFORMS BECAME MORE THE SAME. BRITISH SOLDIERS WORE THE SAME
TYPE OF UNIFORM THE WHOLE TIME. WHY DO YOU THINK THIS WAS?

AFTER THE REVOLUTIONARY WAR HAD BEEN GOING ON A FEW YEARS, WASHINGTON
SET THE UNIFORM FOR AMERICAN SOLDIERS AS A BLUE COAT AND WHITE SHIRT.
THIS WAS TO CONTRAST WITH THE BRITISH SOLDIERS' RED COATS.

JEFFERSON AND HIS WRITING BOX

By mid-1776, leaders of the British colonies in North America were well on the way to declaring that the colonies wanted to be free from England. On June 11, the leaders of the Second Continental Congress in Philadelphia asked five men, including Thomas Jefferson, to write a statement about independence. John Adams, also a member of the group, asked Jefferson to write the first **draft**. Jefferson did so on a **portable** writing desk, which he called his "writing box."

Jefferson often traveled in a carriage from his home near Charlottesville, Virginia, to Philadelphia. He wanted to have a flat surface for writing letters on the long trips, so he designed this box and had it made in Philadelphia. Only a few months later, he wrote the Declaration of Independence on it.

ANALYZE IT!

WHAT DO YOU LEARN ABOUT THOMAS JEFFERSON WHEN YOU LOOK AT THIS DESK? WHAT DO YOU LEARN ABOUT THE TIME PERIOD? WHAT DO YOU THINK HIS NOTE MEANS?

JEFFERSON'S THOUGHTS
ABOUT HIS DESK

JEFFERSON PUT THIS NOTE UNDER THE DESK'S TOP IN 1825: "POLITICS AS WELL AS RELIGION HAS ITS SUPERSTITIONS. THESE, GAINING STRENGTH WITH TIME, MAY, ONE DAY, GIVE IMAGINARY VALUE TO THIS RELIC, FOR ITS GREAT ASSOCIATION WITH THE BIRTH OF THE GREAT CHARTER OF OUR INDEPENDENCE."

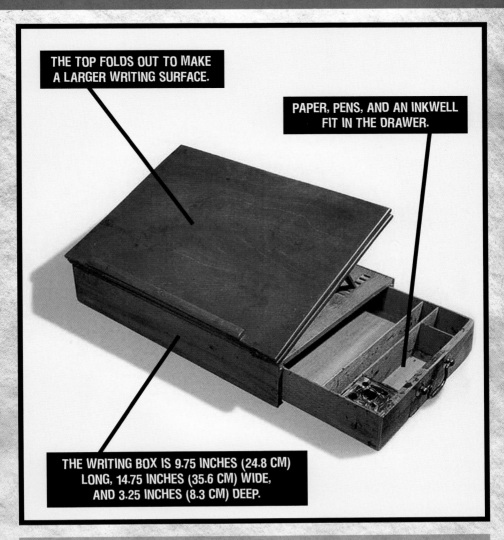

THE TOP FOLDS OUT TO MAKE A LARGER WRITING SURFACE.

PAPER, PENS, AND AN INKWELL FIT IN THE DRAWER.

THE WRITING BOX IS 9.75 INCHES (24.8 CM) LONG, 14.75 INCHES (35.6 CM) WIDE, AND 3.25 INCHES (8.3 CM) DEEP.

JEFFERSON USED THE WRITING BOX ON HIS LAP OR ON A TABLETOP. THE DESK IS MADE OF MAHOGANY WOOD.

WHITNEY'S
COTTON GIN

The Industrial Revolution started in the late 1700s. About this time, machines began taking over jobs that people used to do.

The cotton engine (shortened to "gin") was one of the most important inventions of the Industrial Revolution. Eli Whitney, trying to find an easier way take the seeds out of a certain kind of cotton, invented it in 1793. Before this, enslaved workers did the job by hand. It was slow work that took many people. The cotton gin worked so well that farmers began planting more and more cotton. The size and number of cotton plantations grew. So did the number of slaves the plantation owners kept to do the hard work.

ANALYZE IT!

WHAT DO YOU THINK OF WHEN YOU SEE THIS COTTON GIN? WHAT ELSE WAS HAPPENING IN THE UNITED STATES DURING THE TIME PERIOD IN WHICH IT WAS INVENTED?

ELI WHITNEY

SLAVERY AND
THE COTTON GIN

SLAVERY WAS STILL LEGAL IN THE UNITED STATES WHEN WHITNEY INVENTED THE COTTON GIN. IN 1790, THERE WERE SIX SLAVE STATES; BY 1860, HOWEVER, THERE WERE 15! HISTORIANS BELIEVE THAT THE COTTON GIN HELPED INCREASE THE USE OF SLAVES IN THE SOUTH. PEOPLE IN THE SOUTHERN STATES BROUGHT TENS OF THOUSANDS OF ENSLAVED AFRICANS TO THE COUNTRY BETWEEN 1790 AND 1808.

THIS MODEL OF A COTTON GIN WORKED WITH A HAND CRANK.

SHIP OF
THE LAND

As the United States grew, many people traveled west to settle. They often traveled in covered wagons called prairie schooners. Families packed their food, supplies, and furniture into their wagon for the trip. Young children sometimes rode in the back of the wagon, but older children and adults usually walked alongside it. Horses, mules, or oxen pulled prairie schooners. During stops, people slept on the ground or in the wagon.

Wagons often traveled in large groups called wagon trains. Paid guides took would-be settlers along pathways such as the Oregon Trail and the Santa Fe Trail. The wagon trains moved during the daylight hours, covering up to 20 miles (32 km) a day. A journey from Saint Louis or another midwestern city to the West Coast took about five months.

ANALYZE IT!

WHAT ABOUT THIS PRAIRIE SCHOONER SURPRISES YOU? WHAT WOULD YOU LIKE TO KNOW ABOUT THE PEOPLE WHO USED IT? WHAT DO YOU THINK IT WAS LIKE TO FIGURE OUT WHAT TO TAKE ALONG AND WHAT TO LEAVE BEHIND?

PACKING THE WAGON

FAMILIES HAD TO TAKE ALMOST EVERYTHING THEY NEEDED WITH THEM, AS THERE WERE ONLY A FEW TRADING POSTS ALONG THE WAGON TRAIN TRAILS. THE MAIN FOODS WERE BACON, FLOUR, SUGAR, RICE, BEANS, AND DRIED FRUIT. PEOPLE ALSO TOOK EXTRA WAGON PARTS, FARMING TOOLS, GUNS, AXES, AND KNIVES.

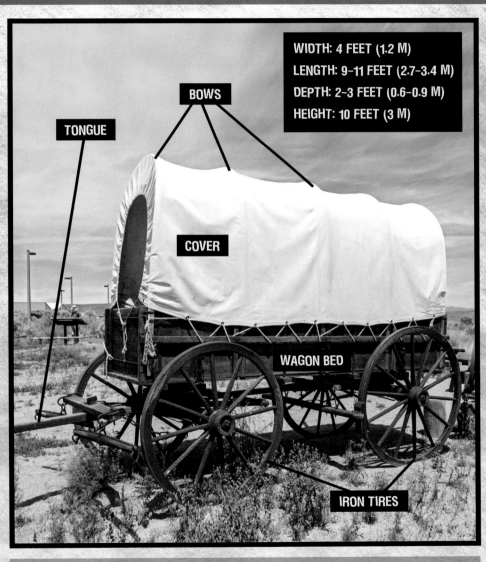

WIDTH: 4 FEET (1.2 M)
LENGTH: 9–11 FEET (2.7–3.4 M)
DEPTH: 2–3 FEET (0.6–0.9 M)
HEIGHT: 10 FEET (3 M)

BOWS

TONGUE

COVER

WAGON BED

IRON TIRES

THE WHITE CANVAS TOP OF A PRAIRIE SCHOONER LOOKED LIKE THE SAIL OF A SHIP CALLED A SCHOONER.

ELLIS ISLAND AND IMMIGRATION CARDS

From 1892 until 1924, Ellis Island was the main entry point to the United States for **immigrants** coming from Europe. The island sits in New York Bay, close to New York City and the Statue of Liberty.

Each immigrant received an inspection card like the one here. A doctor gave them a physical examination to find out if they had any diseases or disabilities. If they were sick and their illness could be cured, new arrivals went to the island's hospital. Those who passed the medical test then answered questions about their reasons for entering the United States. People who passed were allowed into the country. People with incurable illnesses, some disabilities, or criminal records were sent back to the ship on which they had arrived.

ANALYZE IT!

WHAT FEELINGS AND THOUGHTS DO YOU HAVE WHEN YOU LOOK AT THIS INSPECTION CARD? WHAT MIGHT YOU LEARN ABOUT THE PERSON WHO USED THE CARD? WHAT DID THE CARD REPRESENT TO THE PERSON WHO RECEIVED IT?

BY THE NUMBERS

MORE THAN 12 MILLION IMMIGRANTS PASSED THROUGH ELLIS ISLAND BETWEEN 1892 AND 1954. MORE THAN 1 MILLION IMMIGRANTS WENT THROUGH THE ISLAND IN 1907, THE PEAK OF ELLIS ISLAND IMMIGRATION! DOCTORS AT THE ISLAND IMMIGRATION CENTER HAD TO MOVE SO QUICKLY THAT THEY COULD CONDUCT A PHYSICAL EXAM IN 6 SECONDS.

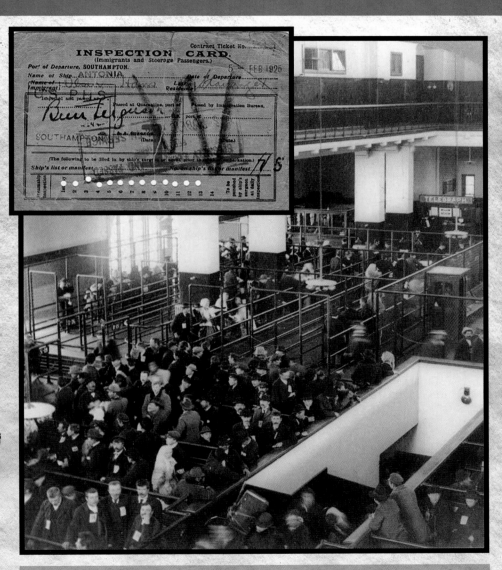

IMMIGRANTS ATTACHED THEIR INSPECTION CARDS TO THEIR CLOTHES. THE CARDS HAD TO BE SHOWN DURING THE INSPECTION PROCESS.

INTO THE
COMPUTER AGE

The word "computer" was first used in 1613 to mean a person who computed, or used math to figure things out. In the 1800s, people began inventing new machines to do math. These machines were also called computers.

The ENIAC (Electronic Numerical Integrator and Computer) in this picture was developed for the US Army during World War II in the 1940s. It used math to work out issues that had to do with weapons. At the time, it was the largest and most powerful computer ever built. Its panels lined three walls of a room that was 50 feet (15.2 m) long and 30 feet (9.1 m) wide. The computer never stopped running. After the war ended, ENIAC was used to solve many other types of math and engineering problems.

ANALYZE IT!

WHERE DO YOUR EYES GO FIRST WHEN YOU LOOK AT THIS ARTIFACT? WHAT DO YOU THINK IT WAS LIKE TO WORK WITH ENIAC? WHAT DOES IT TELL YOU ABOUT HOW COMPUTERS HAVE CHANGED?

AFTER ENIAC

IT WOULD TAKE A BIG GROUP OF PEOPLE ABOUT THREE MONTHS TO DO THE SAME MATH PROBLEMS IT TOOK ENIAC 30 SECONDS TO DO. AFTER ENIAC, COMPUTERS HAVE CONTINUED TO GET SMALLER AND MORE POWERFUL. SOME OF TODAY'S NOTEBOOK COMPUTERS ARE THOUSANDS OF TIMES FASTER AND MORE POWERFUL THAN ENIAC—AND SO MUCH SMALLER!

TWO PIECES OF ENIAC ARE SHOWN ABOVE. THE FULL MACHINE FILLED AN ENTIRE ROOM THAT WAS 50 FEET (15.2 M) LONG!

A SEAT AT THE
COUNTER

In the early 1960s, many restrooms, restaurants, and other places in the United States were still **segregated** by race. Supporters of civil rights for African Americans and others wanted to do away with segregation. They protested it in a number of ways, including **sit-ins.**

The top right photo shows a lunch counter that once stood at a Woolworth store in Greensboro, North Carolina. On February 1, 1960, four African American college students entered, sat down at the counter, tried to order lunch, and were refused. The students were peaceful, but they wouldn't leave until closing. They went back every day, sat down, and tried to order. More people joined them. The lunch counter sit-ins spread throughout the country. In July 1960, African Americans finally were allowed to eat at the Woolworth lunch counter.

ANALYZE IT!

HOW DO YOU THINK THE GREENSBORO FOUR FELT WHEN THEY SAT DOWN AT THIS LUNCH COUNTER?

PEACEFUL PROTESTS

THE COURAGE OF THE GREENSBORO FOUR LED OTHERS IN CITIES AROUND THE COUNTRY TO ORGANIZE SIMILAR PEACEFUL PROTESTS. AS IN GREENSBORO, TELEVISION AND NEWSPAPERS COVERED THE SIT-INS. BY SUMMER 1960, MANY FORMERLY SEGREGATED RESTAURANTS BEGAN ALLOWING AFRICAN AMERICANS TO EAT THERE.

WOOLWORTH LUNCH COUNTER

GREENSBORO FOUR STATUE

David Richmond   Franklin McCain   Ezell Blair, Jr.   Joseph McNeil
(Jibreel Khazan)

EZELL A. BLAIR JR., FRANKLIN E. MCCAIN, JOSEPH A. MCNEIL, AND DAVID L. RICHMOND STARTED THE WOOLWORTH SIT-IN. THEY BECAME KNOWN AS THE GREENSBORO FOUR.

WALL OF
MEMORIES

The Vietnam War took place from 1954 until 1975. US combat troops were involved in the war during much of that time. By 1975, almost 60,000 American soldiers had died or were missing in action in Vietnam. Many more soldiers were wounded.

Vietnam **veterans** and other people left the items shown to the right at the Vietnam Veterans Memorial in Washington, DC. You can see a boot, a flag, a helmet, and more. People have left hundreds of thousands of other artifacts at the memorial, too. Letters, car keys, trophies, old coins, and military hats have been left there, as well as train tickets, packets of candy, fishing equipment, toys, and dolls. The National Park Service collects and saves most of these artifacts.

ANALYZE IT!

WHY DO YOU THINK PEOPLE LEFT THE ITEMS SHOWN AT THE WALL? WHAT DO YOU THINK THEY MEANT TO SOMEONE?

THE VIETNAM VETERANS MEMORIAL

THE VIETNAM VETERANS MEMORIAL IS IN WASHINGTON, DC. THE V-SHAPED BLACK WALL SITS IN A LOW, SLOPING HILLSIDE. IT'S COVERED WITH THE NAMES OF DEAD AND MISSING SOLDIERS. THERE ARE NO OTHER DECORATIONS. THE MEMORIAL IS OPEN ALL DAY, EVERY DAY. MORE THAN 5 MILLION PEOPLE PAY THEIR RESPECTS AT THE MEMORIAL EACH YEAR.

MANY PEOPLE LEAVE ARTIFACTS AT THE VIETNAM VETERANS MEMORIAL. SOMETIMES, THE STORY BEHIND THEM ISN'T OBVIOUS. ONLY THE PERSON OR PEOPLE WHO LEFT THEM KNOW WHY THEY DID SO.

SURVIVAL IN SPACE

On July 20, 1969, US astronaut Neil Armstrong became the first person to walk on the moon. About 20 minutes later, astronaut Edward (Buzz) Aldrin joined him on the moon's surface, where they spent several hours.

Both men wore spacesuits designed so they could survive the flights to and from Earth and the moon's harsh surface. The suits had several layers, and each layer had a specific purpose. The suits had to protect them from extreme temperatures. The middle layer held in the oxygen the astronauts breathed. The outer layer had to be tough enough to withstand cuts and scratches. For their moon walk, the astronauts added extra boots and gloves. A **visor** on the helmet acted as a sunshade. Backpacks held additional breathing equipment.

ANALYZE IT!

WHAT DOES THE SPACE SUIT TELL YOU ABOUT MOVING AROUND IN OUTER SPACE? WHAT QUALITIES WOULD A PERSON NEED TO BE ABLE TO WORK INSIDE A SPACE SUIT? HOW DO YOU THINK IT FELT?

SPACE SUIT
DESIGNERS

SPACE SUIT DESIGNERS HAVE TO UNDERSTAND A LOT ABOUT ENGINEERING AND SPACE. DESIGNERS OFTEN HAVE TO FIGURE OUT HOW TO DO SOMETHING THAT'S NEVER BEEN DONE BEFORE. THEY NEED TO KNOW HOW MATERIALS WILL HOLD UP IN SPACE. DESIGNERS HAVE TO BE CREATIVE AND PAY ATTENTION TO DETAILS AT THE SAME TIME.

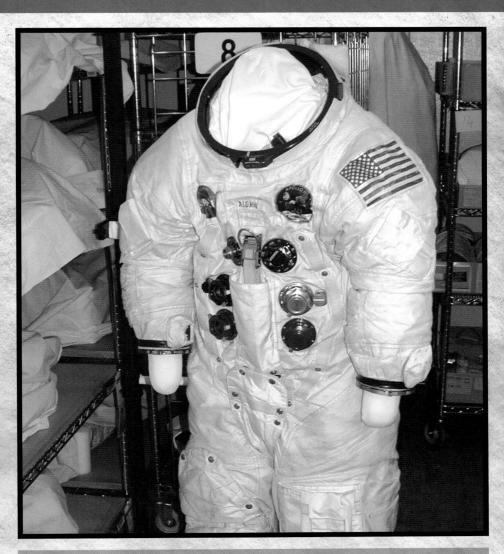

ASTRONAUT BUZZ ALDRIN'S SPACE SUIT FROM THE FIRST MOON LANDING IS SHOWN. THE SPACE SUIT AND BACKPACK WEIGHED 180 POUNDS (81.6 KG) ON EARTH, BUT THEY WEIGHED 30 POUNDS (13.6 KG) ON THE MOON.

SEPTEMBER 11, 2001

September 11, 2001, was a terrible day for the United States. **Terrorists** from a group called al-Qaeda took over four airplanes that were in flight. They flew two planes into the World Trade Center towers in New York City and one plane into the Pentagon building in Washington, DC. Passengers on the fourth plane struggled with the terrorists and flew the plane into the ground near Shanksville, Pennsylvania. Nearly 3,000 people died on the planes and on the ground.

Many artifacts were recovered from the crash sites. Some are tiny, such as shards of glass from World Trade Center windows. Some are huge. The fire truck shown was parked near the World Trade Center when it collapsed. It's badly damaged, with its metal ripped apart like paper.

ANALYZE IT!

THE EMERGENCY WORKERS WHO WENT TO THE WORLD TRADE CENTER SITE WANTED TO RESCUE PEOPLE. WHY DO YOU THINK THEY DID THAT? HOW DO YOU THINK THEY FELT WHEN THEY SAW THE SCENE?

THE SEPTEMBER 11
MEMORIAL

THE 9/11 MEMORIAL AND MUSEUM IS LOCATED AT THE SITE OF THE WORLD TRADE CENTER IN NEW YORK CITY. THE MEMORIAL OPENED IN 2011 AND THE MUSEUM OPENED IN 2014. IT HONORS THOSE WHO DIED IN THE ATTACKS ON SEPTEMBER 11, 2001, AND SIX OTHERS WHO DIED IN A WORLD TRADE CENTER BOMBING IN 1993.

CELL PHONES AND DEVICES

FIRE TRUCK

MANY FIRST RESPONDERS, INCLUDING FIREFIGHTERS, DIED AT THE WORLD TRADE CENTER SCENE AFTER GOING THERE TO HELP.

ARTIFACTS OF THE
FUTURE

Some day in the future, the things we use now will be artifacts. Archaeologists or historians may examine our possessions and our trash to learn about the early 21st century. They may look at our toys, our tools, and even our medical devices to learn about us. What might they find?

One fairly new medical device is a full or partial **exoskeleton.** These devices can help a person walk. The military is also developing exoskeletons that might be able to make soldiers stronger. People in the future might look at one of today's exoskeletons and wonder what role, or part, it played in our lives. Will they think we tried to help people? Or will they think we were warlike? Maybe both!

ANALYZE IT!

HOW MIGHT FUTURE PEOPLE VIEW THINGS YOU USE TODAY? WHAT MIGHT SOMEONE THINK ABOUT A SMARTPHONE? WHAT INFORMATION MIGHT OUR GARBAGE GIVE ABOUT OUR LIFESTYLE?

MAKING MISTAKES

EVEN TRAINED HISTORIANS AND SCIENTISTS SOMETIMES MAKE MISTAKES. PEOPLE HAVE IDENTIFIED ARTIFACTS AS COMING FROM A CERTAIN TIME AND PLACE ONLY TO FIND LATER THAT THEY CAME FROM ANOTHER TIME OR LOCATION. SOMETIMES THEY MISIDENTIFY THINGS AS HAVING A COMPLETELY DIFFERENT PURPOSE! IT'S IMPORTANT TO KEEP LEARNING, EVEN ABOUT THE THINGS WE THINK WE KNOW ABOUT.

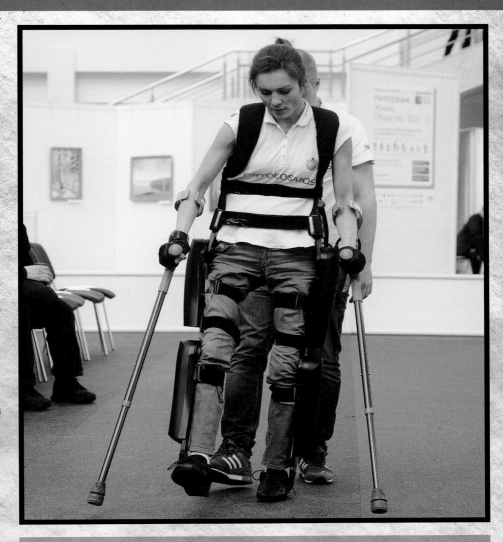

AN EXOSKELETON MAY BE ABLE TO GIVE SOMEONE THE ABILITY TO WALK.

GLOSSARY

analyze: to find out what something is made of

culture: the beliefs and ways of life of a group of people

document: a formal piece of writing

draft: the first try of a piece of writing

exoskeleton: a hard outer structure that gives support

immigrant: one who comes to a country to settle there

portable: easy to move

rebellion: a fight to overthrow a government

segregate: to force separation of races or classes

sit-in: a protest in which people sit or stay in a place and won't leave until they're heard

terrorist: one who uses violence and fear to challenge an authority

veteran: someone who fought in a war

visor: a front part of a helmet, made of see-through material, and used to protect the face or eyes

FOR MORE INFORMATION

BOOKS

Mullenbach, Cheryl. *The Industrial Revolution for Kids.* Chicago, Illinois: Chicago Review Press, 2014.

Partridge, Elizabeth. *Boots on the Ground: America's War in Vietnam.* New York, New York: Viking Books for Young Readers, 2018.

Peterson, Megan Cooley. *The National Air and Space Museum.* North Mankato, Minnesota: Capstone Press, 2017.

WEBSITES

9/11 Museum & Memorial
collection.911memorial.org
The September 11 Memorial and Museum honors the deceased, the survivors, and the heroes from the attacks on September 11, 2001.

National Park Service, Ellis Island
nps.gov/elis/learn/historyculture/collections.htm
This website covers the artifacts and records that are housed in the museum collection of the Statue of Liberty National Monument and Ellis Island.

Jamestown Settlement & American Revolution Museum at Yorktown
historyisfun.org
The website covers both museums and includes artifacts from the first settlement at Jamestown through the American Revolution.

INDEX